"This biblically inspired book belongs on every child's bookshelf as well as on every nursing-home bedside table. Read it to someone you love – it will make you feel like putting your arms around each other and celebrating God's love for eternity."
VALERIE BELL, CEO of Awana Cubs International

"We have had many adventures as a family with Joni! But, as she so winsomely reminds us here, these are echoes of a greater party we are called to. How wonderful to have a book like this!"
KRISTYN GETTY, Hymnwriter and Author

"I love this book and can't wait to read it to my grandkids! It's beautifully written and full of whimsy, and it brings the mysteries of heaven to each page!"
BOB GOFF, Author of *Love Does*

"I so appreciate Joni's passion to share the gospel with children, and this powerful book about heaven will be an encouragement to countless boys and girls."
REESE KAUFFMAN, President of Child Evangelism Fellowship

"A captivating book – winsome for kids and inspiring for the adults who read it with them."
MANDY ARIOTO, President and CEO of MOPS International

"Joni loves kids, and they love Joni. In this book she introduces young ones to heaven and tells them how to embrace God's invitation to spend eternity with her Savior."
ROBERT AND NANCY DEMOSS WOLGEMUTH, Authors and Speakers; Founder of Revive Our Hearts

"If ever our world needed a joyous reminder of the hope of heaven, it's now. This is a gloriously rendered invitation to the Lord's eternal party that will be a joy to share."
DIANE DOKKO KIM, Disability Ministry Advocate and Author of *Unbroken Faith: Spiritual Recovery for the Special-Needs Parent*

"The title is long. The book is short. The author is Joni! Help your children (and grandchildren) long for the appearing of the Lord Jesus by reading them this book. Read like you mean it – the way Joni would."
JOHN PIPER, Lead Teacher at desiringGod.org

"This is one of the best children's books I've ever read about the best promise ever given, the promise of heaven coming to earth so that earth becomes heaven. Reading it makes me want to say, 'Come quickly Lord Jesus!'"
NANCY GUTHRIE, Author of *What Every Child Should Know about Prayer*

The Awesome Super Fantastic Forever Party
© Joni Eareckson Tada / Catalina Echeverri 2022. Reprinted 2023.

Illustrated by Catalina Echeverri | Design & Art Direction by André Parker

"The Good Book For Children" is an imprint of The Good Book Company Ltd
North America: thegoodbook.com UK: thegoodbook.co.uk Australia: thegoodbook.com.au
New Zealand: thegoodbook.co.nz India: thegoodbook.co.in

Published in association with the literary agency of Wolgemuth & Associates, Inc.

ISBN: 9781784987534 | JOB-007516 | Printed in India

The AWESOME SUPER FANTASTIC FOREVER PARTY

written by:
JONI EARECKSON TADA

illustrated by:
CATALINA ECHEVERRI

Have you ever received
an invitation...

To a birthday party?

To watch a
football game?

To a big wedding?

The best invitations are to unforgettable
events with amazing people.

Jesus loved giving invitations. And his most wonderful invitation of all was this:

Everyone who believes in me as their King and Rescuer will have life, with me, forever.

He was inviting
people to heaven.

But... hmm... isn't heaven a place where I will just live on a cloud, wear a funny white robe, and play a harp? It sounds a bit... not exciting. YAWN.

But then some people say heaven is a place where I could dive with dolphins... ride the biggest water slide in all the universe...

and eat all the chocolate-chip pancakes I want...

That would be great! For a few years. But then what? Do I really want to eat chocolate-chip pancakes all day and end up with a stomachache forever?!

Jesus talked a lot about the life
after this life — but he never once
mentioned people sitting on clouds.
Or eating pancakes.

The things he talked
about were much more
amazing things.

So, what's the TRUTH
about heaven?!

First, Jesus said that one day heaven will be here.

When Jesus comes back to this world, he will bring heaven with him. Heaven and earth will join together.

Which means that the world will be perfect.

What's your favorite place in the world?
In the new earth, it'll be even better.
Nothing will get broken or go wrong.

You'll get to do amazing things.
You might...

Take care of exotic
animals.

Climb to the top of
snowy mountains.

Meet all the stars
that Jesus made.

And in this perfect heaven-on-earth,
you will be perfect, too!

Jesus will give you a
new HEART.

That means no more sin. You won't want
to steal cookies, be mean to your friend,
or pretend you've brushed your teeth when
really you haven't.

Everyone else will have a new heart, too.

There will be no arguing or hurting —
only peace and friendship.

Life will be like standing
under a waterfall of happiness!

And Jesus will give you a new BODY.

It will be shining and splendorous, and you'll run faster and be stronger than you thought possible. Blind people will see, lame people will dance, deaf people will hear, and people whose minds sometimes struggle will enjoy minds that work just right, all the time.

And on this new earth,

with our new hearts and new bodies...

We'll get to live in a new CITY – the new Jerusalem, a sparkling city where Jesus has prepared a home just for you.

Wow! And we haven't even got to the best thing about the place we're invited to. The best thing will be...

JESUS.

Jesus is the All-Time, Undisputed Lord and Champion! He will rule with Kindness and wisdom, and everyone will bow down and happily shout,

"Jesus deserves to rule as King!"

Jesus is the only one who has paid for our sins, by dying on the cross. He is the only one who has left death for dead, by rising back to life. He is the only one who can invite us to this amazing party. WOW!

So everyone in the new Jerusalem will pile praise after praise on Jesus. We will thank him for rescuing us and for giving us the joy of being at his awesome super fantastic forever party!

Trees will clap their hands
in praise to Jesus...

grain in the fields will wave in delight...

mountains will shout... and stars
will sing along with us in worship!
Everyone and everything will be brimming
over with joy for the Lord Jesus.

But hang on... the problem with
parties is that they finish.

The fun

has

to

stop.

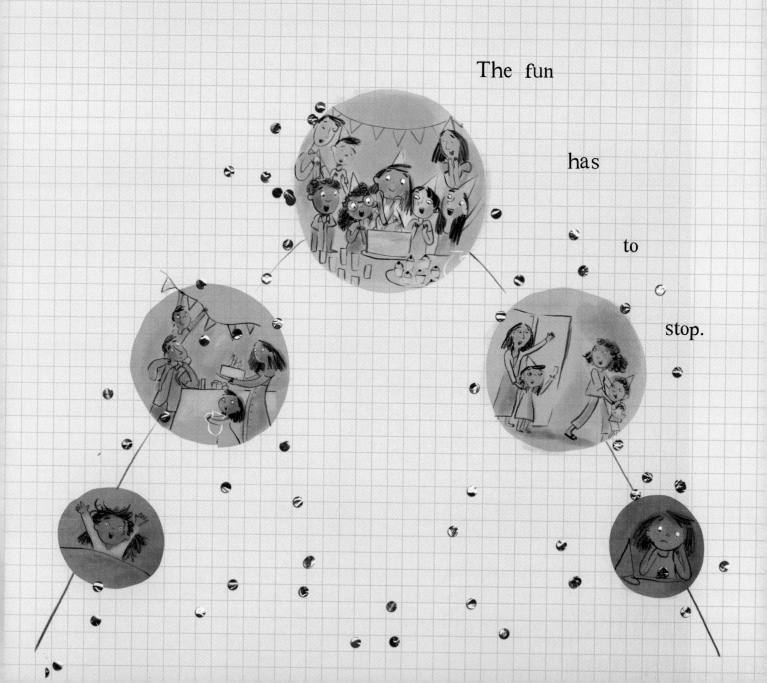

But not this one! This party goes on forever. There'll always be a tomorrow, and every tomorrow will be better than every yesterday. Each day we'll get to enjoy new things, see new places, meet new people, and learn amazing new truths about God.

The best invitations are to unforgettable events with amazing people. And this is the greatest invitation of all.

Now, when you get an invitation, you have to reply to say whether you're coming or not.

How do you say "Yes!" to Jesus' invitation?

Yes!

By telling him that you want him to be your King and Rescuer. Then you can know that your name is on his eternal party list called "the Book of Life."

And then you can invite your friends
and family to be there with Jesus too.
Everyone is invited!

When the very last person on Jesus' list replies and says "Yes!" to him... that's when Jesus will show up, suddenly, here, with ALL his friends who have been waiting with him in heaven after their lives in this world ended.

And then everything will change, and all Jesus' friends will be together, and the eternal party will start!

And so there's one more thing we can do as we look forward to having new hearts and new bodies in the new heaven-on-earth, with Jesus forever.

We can send our own invitation to Jesus.

It's an invitation that is on the last page of the last chapter of the last book of the Bible, Revelation.

It's there three times. (It must be important!)
So, let's say it together...

"PLEASE COME QUICKLY, JESUS!"

HOW DO WE KNOW ABOUT
THE AWESOME SUPER FANTASTIC FOREVER PARTY?

I wrote this book because I love Jesus, and I want others to love him too. I also live in a wheelchair and am looking forward to the wonderful day described in Isaiah 35:10: "They will enter Zion with singing; everlasting joy will crown their heads. Gladness and joy will overtake them, and sorrow and sighing will flee away." The Bible promises that one day I will rise from my wheelchair and enter heaven happy and dancing.

Being with Jesus is what will make heaven feel so heavenly. There, we will have new hearts that will perfectly love him (Jeremiah 24:7). We will experience life without any trace of anger, resentment, fear, or envy because heaven is our home of righteousness (2 Peter 3:13).

Revelation 21:3-4 says that when Jesus returns, God will make a new earth free of decay and disasters. Heaven and earth will be joined together (Revelation 21:2; Isaiah 65:17-19). We will be perfectly suited to live in this new heaven-and-earth because God will give us new bodies (1 Corinthians 15:35-44). We cannot say exactly what our bodies will look like, but they will be perfect.

This is why this book ends with the same invitation as the Bible does: for Jesus to come back soon (Revelation 22:20)!

Enjoy all of the award-winning "Tales That Tell The Truth" series:

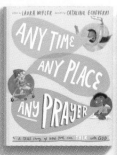